Martin Luther

The Table Talk of Doctor Martin Luther

Martin Luther

The Table Talk of Doctor Martin Luther

ISBN/EAN: 9783337127183

Printed in Europe, USA, Canada, Australia, Japan

Cover: Foto ©Lupo / pixelio.de

More available books at **www.hansebooks.com**

TABLE TALK.

"I WOULD NOT PART WITH MY SMALL SKILL IN MUSIC FOR MUCH."—*Page* 116.

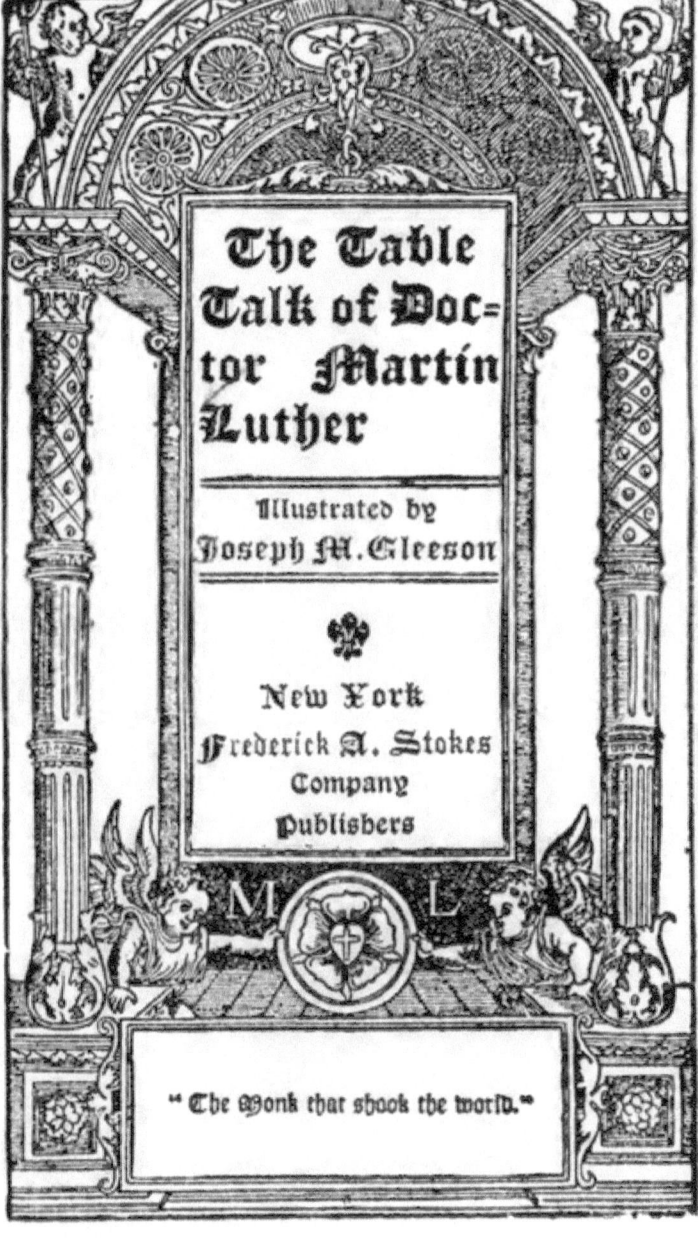

The Table Talk of Doctor Martin Luther

Illustrated by Joseph M. Gleeson

New York
Frederick A. Stokes Company
Publishers

"The Monk that shook the world."

COPYRIGHT, 1893, BY
FREDERICK A. STOKES COMPANY.

CONTENTS.

	PAGE
INTRODUCTION	7

BOOK I.

OF THE WORKS OF GOD	21
OF THE WORD OF GOD	27
OF JESUS CHRIST	35
OF THE LAW AND THE GOSPEL	39
OF THE CHURCH	41
OF PREACHING AND PREACHERS	45
OF CONFESSION AND ABSOLUTION	55
THE LORD'S SUPPER	57
GOOD WORKS	61
OF THE DEVIL	63
PRAYER	69

BOOK II.

	PAGE
OF DEATH	73
OF THE RESURRECTION OF THE DEAD AND LIFE ETERNAL	77
OF MARRIAGE	81
OF THE JEWS	87
OF ECCLESIASTICAL LEGENDS	93
THE WORLD AND ITS WAYS	97
OF PRINCES AND RULERS	105
OF THE USE OF LEARNING	111
OF COMEDIES	113
OF THE POWER OF MUSIC	115
OF SINGING	117
OF GERMANY	119
OF LANGUAGES	123
OF THE SCHOOLS AND UNIVERSITIES OF GERMANY	127
OF THE TURKS	131
OF THE HEROES AND WISE MEN OF ANTIQUITY	133
OF THE FATHERS AND DOCTORS OF THE CHURCH	137

INTRODUCTION.

LUTHER is the national hero of the German people. No king or statesman, not even their great poets Goethe and Schiller, have such a place in the hearts of the Germans as "Doctor Martin Luther." The feeling cherished towards him is rather a personal affection towards a familiar friend, than the distant admiration felt for a great man who has been dead for more than three hundred years. This is due in no small measure to his Letters and to his Table Talk, from which we offer a few selections in this volume. Luther was in the habit of talking much to the friends who gathered round him at the evening meal in his home at Wittenberg. In these talks he revealed himself with a frankness which has few parallels in history. Fortunately for posterity, there was a Boswell present in the person of John Goldschmidt, or, to give him his Latinized name, *Aurifaber*, who made copious notes of the talk of the master. Not satisfied with what he heard himself, he applied to other friends who had been longer guests at Luther's table than himself; and from their recollections he supplemented his own. He did not publish the collection immediately after Luther's death; and he appears to have felt some hesitation about publication.

This is not surprising; for Luther had uttered a most energetic protest against the posthumous publication of his remains. But in the year 1566 the book appeared, and *Aurifaber* said in the preface, that he felt he could no longer with a good conscience withhold from the world the precious treasure of which he was the possessor. The publication may have been something of an indiscretion; for it proclaimed to the whole world, words which had been carelessly uttered in the society of trusted friends; and there is always a certain injustice in such revelations. But Luther's character was able to bear the fierce light thus cast upon it. His faults are visible enough in these conversations. He is often impatient and unreasonable. Sometimes he is coarse, and there are expressions in his talk which seem to border on irreverence, although here, perhaps, the fault is quite as much with the modern reader as with Luther. But when all abatements have been made, the Luther of these conversations is one of the most attractive characters of history. What love and tenderness to the weak! what courage in denouncing wrong, which indeed is but the reverse side of his great pity for the weak! Another quality that strikes us in Dr. Aurifaber's recollections is Luther's unfailing sense of humour. Reformers are usually deficient in humour. Their earnestness seldom permits them to laugh. Luther was the most earnest man of his century, and lived in more earnest times than any Europe had witnessed since the close of the first century. But his merry laugh rings through the entire solemn drama of his life. He relieved himself and others by permitting himself glimpses at the ludicrous aspects which human nature presents even in the transaction of its most solemn and momentous matters.

Luther's reputation has indeed gained rather than lost through the somewhat indiscreet publication of his familiar "Table Talk." He has been the subject of much obloquy, which is hardly to be wondered at. He was the leader of a fierce theological debate, and he never spared his foes. He was the cause of a schism in the Church of Germany which, however inevitable, was the occasion of great evils. He was indeed from his position the natural mark for the hatred of opponents. But as time has gone on, Germans of all shades of opinions have been irresistibly fascinated by the strong tender man, a German Saint Christopher, who seems to bend over them with eyes of infinite love and pity, like the presiding genius of their nation. Theological bitterness is not extinct in Germany

any more than in England, but even those who profess a different theology from Luther, or no theology at all, now recognize the greatness of Luther. Ferdinand Christian Von Baur, the distinguished leader of the Tübingen school, writes thus of Luther in his "Church History:" "Every one in whose veins German blood flows must recognize in Luther a German man in whom, as in no other, the German character was exhibited in its purest and noblest features." One, who might have been expected to be more hostile to Luther than Baur, the eminent Roman Catholic professor, Dr. Döllinger, of Munich, has also expressed his sense of Luther's greatness with no less justice than generosity. "Luther is the most powerful man of the people, the most popular character whom Germany has ever possessed. In the spirit of this German man, the greatest among his contemporaries, Protestant doctrine arose. Before the superiority of his genius and his creative energy, the most aspiring and energetic portion of German people bowed the knee in humility and faith. In this man, in whom power was combined with insight, they recognized their master, and by his thoughts they lived. He seemed to them the hero in whom their nation had become incarnate." On another occasion Dr. Döllinger wrote of Luther:—" Luther's supereminent greatness of soul, and his marvellous many-sidedness made him the man of his time and the man of his people. There never was a German who understood his people with such intuitive perception, and who was so understood—I may say drunk in—by his people as this Augustinian monk of Wittenberg. He held the mind and the spirit of the Germans in hand as a musician holds his lyre." One more example may be given of German reverence for Luther. Heine was a Jew by birth, and a religious sceptic, and as a critic he often employed his unrivalled mastery of gibes and sarcasms in sneering away German reputations. But of Luther he wrote:—" Honour to Luther! Everlasting honour to the dear man to whom we owe the recovery of our noblest rights, and through whose labours we live to-day! It becomes us ill to complain of the narrowness of his views. The dwarf who stands upon the shoulders of the giant may certainly see farther, especially if he puts on spectacles; but he cannot bring to the prospect the lofty emotion and the giant heart of the other. It becomes us the less to judge his faults severely, as his very faults were of more service to us than the virtues of a thousand others. The fine discernment of Erasmus, and the gentle-

Introduction.

ness of Melanchthon, had never done so much for us as the divine brutality of Brother Martin."

It is exactly four hundred years since Luther was born, and during the present autumn Germany has been showing its undiminished interest in him by numerous celebrations, while the German press has been teeming with publications on his life and works. The interest has extended to England, and we have thought that the present selection from his "Table Talk" might be acceptable to English readers. The edition we have used in making this translation is that of Dr. Förstemann.[1]

---

[1] D. Martin Luther's Tischreden oder Colloquia. Nach Aurifaber's erster Ausgabe, mit sorgfältiger Vergleichung sowohl der Stangwaldschen als der Selneccer'schen Redaction herausgegeben und erlautert von Karl Eduard Förstemann, Doctor der Theologie. Leipzig, 1844.

Portions of the "Table Talk" have been already translated into English. A Captain Henry Bell, who lived in the reign of Charles I., made a translation which was submitted to Archbishop Laud, then in prison. After many delays, Captain Bell received a letter from the archbishop's chaplain, Dr. Bray, approving of his book. "He sent me," writes Captain Bell, "both the said original book and my translation, and caused his chaplain, the said doctor, to tell me that he would make it known unto his Majesty what an excellent piece of work I had translated, and that he would procure an order from his Majesty to have the said translation printed, and to be dispersed throughout the whole kingdom." The translation which gained the approval of Laud was afterwards ordered to be printed by the House of Commons, on the 24th of February, 1646.

Introduction. 17

Mr. William Hazlitt translated with great spirit a portion of the " Table Talk," and his translation is now one of the volumes of Bohn's Standard Library.

J. G.

October, 1883.

BOOK I.

OF THE WORKS OF GOD.

GOD could become exceedingly rich, were He so minded. Were He, for example, to come to the Pope, to the Emperor, to kings, bishops, doctors, citizens, and farmers, and say to them: "You shall die this very hour, unless you give me a hundred thousand gulden;" all would reply, "I will give them willingly, if I may but live." But we are such low, thankless fellows, that we do not give him so much as a *Deo gratias* for all the great benefits which we daily receive in such abundance of His free goodness and mercy. Is not it a shame? Were He more sparing with His gifts, we should be more thankful to Him. If, for example, He caused every man to be born with one leg or one foot, and gave him the other leg seven years later. And were He to give to man one hand in his fourteenth year, and his second hand in his twentieth year, we should then better recognize His gifts and benefits, and value them more. Now has He given us a whole sea full of His word. He gives us all manner of languages and liberal arts. All sorts of books can be bought cheap; and there are learned men in abundance who are able to teach in an orderly and correct manner, so that a boy, if not altogether a dunce, may learn more in a single year than in former times could have been learned in many years. The arts are now so cheap that they must almost go begging for bread. Woe be to us that we are so lazy, negligent, and unthankful! When Dr. Martin saw the cattle in the field he said: "There go our preachers, the bearers of milk, of butter, of cheese, and of wool, who daily preach faith in God, and tell us to put our trust in Him, as our Father who cares for us and nourishes us (Matt. vi. 2)."

* * *

Towards evening there came into the Doctor's garden two birds which had made their nests there. But they were often frightened when any one passed near. Then said the Doctor: "Ah, you dear little bird, do not fly away, I am heartily well disposed towards you, would you only believe it." In like manner have we no trust in God, who has nevertheless always shown us every kindness. He who has given His Son for us will not strike us dead.

* * * *

God alone and not wealth nourishes and upholds us. Riches make people proud and lazy. At Venice, where there are the richest people in the world, there was a terrible famine within our recollection, and the Venetians were obliged to appeal to the Turks for help. They sent twenty-four galleys laden with corn, which, when they were about to enter the harbour of Venice, sunk before the eyes of the people. Wealth cannot satisfy hunger, but rather makes the dearth greater. For where there are many rich people, things are dearer. Moreover, money makes no man joyful, but rather makes him downcast, and fills him with cares. For riches, as Christ says, are like thorns, and they prick men. Yet is the world so foolish as to seek for all its joy in riches.

OF THE WORD OF GOD.

DID not learn my theology all at once. I was constrained by my perplexities to search deeper and deeper
The Scripture cannot be understood except through perplexities and temptations. St. Paul had a devil that beat him with fists, and drove him by means of his temptations to the diligent study of Scripture. I had the Pope, the Universities, and all the learned, and by these the devil had me in his

grip. But they hunted me into the Bible so that I read it diligently, and at length I attained to a true understanding of the Word of God.

* * *

The Holy Scriptures are full of Divine gifts and virtues. The heathen books taught nothing of faith, hope, and love, for they knew nothing of them. They look only to the present, and to what man can feel and grasp with his reason. But of faith and hope in God they cannot speak. It is in the Psalms and in the Book of Job that we shall find such counsels, for they treat of faith, hope, patience, and prayer. In a word, Holy Scripture is the highest and best Book of God, full of comfort for every season of temptation.

* * *

Dr. Justin Jonas once told Dr.

Martin Luther of a noble in Meissen who gave himself to the amassing of gold and treasure, and was so blinded that he cared nothing for the five Books of Moses. This man said to the Duke John Frederic, who had been discussing with him about the Gospel: "Sir, the Gospel is nothing to your Grace." Luther then told this fable: "The lion made a great feast, and he invited all the beasts, and among the others, a sow was invited. And when all manner of costly dishes were set before the guests, the sow asked: 'Is there any bran there?' Even so," said Luther, "is it with the Epicureans of to-day. We preachers place before them, in our churches, the most costly dainties, eternal blessedness, the forgiveness of sins, and the grace of God. But they, like swine, turn up their snouts and grub for money."

* * *

The words of the Lord Christ are full of power, and have hands and feet, and they repel all the assaults which the wisdom and cunning of wise men can make. This we see in the Gospels.

* * *

Saint Jerome, who first corrected and improved the version of the Seventy, afterwards translated the Bible from the Hebrew into Latin, and this is the translation which we still use in our churches. He has done well enough for one, *Nulla enim privata persona tantum efficere potuisset.* But he would have done better had he got one or two learned men to aid him in the translation. Then had the Holy Ghost been more powerful according to the word of Christ. "For where two or three are gathered together in my name, there am I in the midst of them"

(Matt. xviii. 21). Translators should not be alone, for not to one man will the fitting word always occur.

The art of the scholastic theologians, with its speculations on Holy Scripture, is nothing but pure vanity, and the thoughts of human reason. I have read much in Buonaventura, but he made me almost deaf. I desired greatly to understand how God is united with my soul; but I could learn nothing from such writings on the subject. They say much of the union of the understanding and the will, but it is vain phantasy and fanaticism. This is the true speculative and the much more practical theology: Believe on Christ, and do what thou art bound to do in thy calling.

* * * *

Dr. Luther once said: "Had I known at first, before I began to write, what I now know, that people are so hostile to the Word of God, and determined to oppose it, I should certainly have held my tongue. I should never have been so bold as to attack the Pope and almost all men, and incense them against me. I thought that they sinned through ignorance and human frailty. I did not understand that they purposely kept down the Word of God. But God drew me on in my blindness, just as men blind a horse that he may run the better."

* * * *

I believe that the beautiful fables of Æsop arose in this way. When the Emperor Julian, who was a Mameluke and an apostate Christian, forbade men to read the Scriptures or to teach them within his empire, two pious bishops, as the church histories tell us, became schoolmasters, and taught the young boys in the schools. They amused them with such fables, and showed them Truth clad in a fair garment of flowers.

OF JESUS CHRIST.

ALL the wisdom of the world is childish folly in comparison with the knowledge of Christ. For what is more marvellous than the great and unspeakable mystery that the Son of God, the image of the Eternal Father, took our human nature, and was in form and countenance like any other man? In Nazareth he would help his father Joseph to build houses; for Joseph was a carpenter; and Christ was called the carpenter's son. What will the people of Nazareth think at the Day of Judgment, when they shall see Christ in His Divine majesty. They will say to Him: "Lord, didst Thou not help to build my house? How hast Thou come to this great honour?"

* * *
*

When Jesus was born He wept and cried like any other child. Mary had to tend Him, and to give Him suck as the Church teacheth. When He returned to Nazareth after the death of Herod, He was subject to his parents, and He would often fetch bread and water and other things for them. Mary would often say to Him: "My dear little Jesus, where hast Thou been? Canst Thou not remain at home?"

* * *
*

We cannot vex the devil more than by teaching, preaching, and singing of the child Jesus. Therefore I am always well pleased when we sing loud and solemnly in the church : *Et homo factus est;* and, *Verbum caro factum est.* The devil cannot bear to hear these words, but flees miles away, for he knows well what they signify.

* * * *

"Many of the dead are forgotten, can you not also forget the dead Christ?" These words were spoken by a Jew, and very devilish words they are. Yes, dear devil, but there are the words, "Sit Thou at My right hand." And therefore must Christ be preached —His sufferings and His death—as long as the world stands.

* * * *

Christ our High Priest is gone into the

heavens. He "sitteth at the right hand of the Father, and continually maketh intercession for us" (Rom. viii. 34). In these words St. Paul gives a picture of Christ in very beautiful and glorious words. In His Death He is a sacrifice; in His Resurrection a conqueror; in His Ascension a king; in His Intercession a high priest; for by the law of Moses the high priest alone entered the *Sancta Sanctorum* and prayed for the people.

OF THE LAW AND THE GOSPEL.

 WILL have none of Moses with his law, for he is the enemy of the Lord Christ. If he summons me for judgment, I will dismiss him and say, "In God's name no, here standeth Christ." At the Day of Judgment Moses will look to me and say: "Thou didst understand me rightly, and didst make a very proper distinction." And we shall be very good friends.

The law is given to the proud, for

example to the City N. N. and others. Likewise to hypocrites, who desire it, and are pleased to have many laws. But grace is promised to the humble, to those of troubled and tormented hearts, for to them does forgiveness of sin belong. M. Nicolaus, Cordatus, Philip and I belong to Grace.

* * *

Where the true Gospel is, there is poverty; as it is written, "I am sent to preach the gospel to the poor" (Isa. xi. 1). In former times people were willing to bestow in gift whole cloisters, now they will give nothing. Superstition, false teaching, and hypocrisy give money enough. Truth goeth a-begging.

* * *

A lie is like a snowball, the longer one rolls it the larger it grows.

OF THE CHURCH.

AN olive-tree grows for two hundred years and bears fruit. It is a fine image of the Church. Its oil signifies the love and friendliness of the gospel. Wine again signifieth the doctrine of the law. And there is so great natural affinity between the vine and the olive-tree, that when the vine is engrafted on the olive-tree it brings forth both wine and oil. So the Church, when engrafted on the people, teacheth both gospel and law, and has of both fruit.

* * *

The amaranth is a flower which grows in the month of August. It is more stalk than flower, is easily broken off, and grows in a joyful and pleasant fashion. When all other flowers decay, this flower, if sprinkled with water, becomes again fair and green, so that in winter garlands are made of it. It is called amaranth because it neither withers nor decays.

* * *

I know not anything more like the Church than this most lovely flower. For although the Church bathes her garments in the blood of the Lamb, as we read in Genesis and in the Apocalypse, and is of a red colour, yet is she more fair than any state or assembly upon the earth. The Son of God loves her as His bride, and in her alone has He pleasure and joy. To her alone does His heart cling, and He rejects and loathes all others who despise or falsify His gospel.

* * *

Moreover, the Church willingly suffers herself to be plucked and broken off, that is, she is obedient to God and submissive under the cross.

* * *

We tell our Lord God that if He will have His Church, He must uphold it. We cannot uphold it for Him, and were it possible for us to do so, we should soon become the proudest asses under heaven. But God says, "I say it, I do it." It is God alone that speaks, and He does nothing according to the mind of the ungodly, or as they hold to be good and right.

OF PREACHING AND PREACHERS.

DR. MARTIN LUTHER said to a pastor, "When you are about to preach, speak with God and say, 'Dear Lord God, I will preach to Thy honour, and speak of Thee. Thee I will adore, and praise Thy name, although I cannot do it so well as I should wish to do.' And do not look at Philip, or at me, or at any of the learned men, but reckon yourself to be the most learned when you speak of God from the pulpit. I have never allowed myself to be shocked by the idea that cannot preach well, but I have often I been filled with fear because I had to speak of the majesty of God and for Him. Therefore be strong and pray."

* * *
*

The faults of a preacher are quickly observed. If a pious preacher has ten virtues and but one fault, the one fault obscures all his virtues. So evil is our world. Dr. Jonas has all the virtues of a preacher, but because he often hems, the people cannot endure the good man.

* * *
*

Some preachers torment their hearers with long sermons. Hearing is a delicate thing, and we soon become tired of a subject. Dr. Pomner always quotes, as an excuse for his long sermons, the words of St. John, " He that is of God heareth God's word" (John viii. 47). But moderation is good in all things.

* * *

Cursed be those preachers who in the churches deal with difficult, subtle matters, and bring such before the people. They seek their own honour, and wish to give pleasure to one or two ambitious hearers. When I preach I let myself down to the lowest : I don't see the doctors and the magistrates, of whom there are about forty, but I look at the crowd of young people, the children and the servants, who are there in hundreds or thousands. To them I preach and direct my words, for they have need of my words. If the others do not wish to listen to me, the door stands open !

Theology consists in use and practice, not in speculation or in examination of the things of God by the reason. Every art, whether applied to household affairs or to government, loses itself and becomes unprofitable when it indulges in speculations.

* * *

A jurist may be a rogue, but a theologian must be a man of piety. A jurist has to deal only with the affairs of this temporal world, but a theologian has to deal with things spiritual and eternal which have been committed to him by God. His heaven and all His gifts and treasures, forgiveness of sins, righteousness—these have been committed to the theologian. Piety becomes such a trust. For God says, "Whose soever sins ye remit, him I receive as my child."

* * *

Jurists, theologians, and physicians may counsel, absolve, and help. But what is said to such persons ought to be kept secret by them.

* * *
*

There is continual hatred between the clergy and the laity, and not without reason; for unbridled mobs of peasants, citizens, nobles, and especially the princes and lords, refuse to listen to reproof. But it is the office of the preacher to reprove those who live in open sin, and who offend against the Ten Commandments of God, whether of the first or of the second Table. This is very distasteful to men, and they watch with very sharp eyes those preachers who do their duty faithfully.

* * *
*

At court these rules should be observed. We must cry aloud and accuse.

If we are not heard the first time, we must ask again. For neither modesty nor the gospel suits the court, and we must complain and importune. We must place Moses with his horns in the court, and not Christ, who is mild and friendly. Therefore I counsel my pastors to complain at court of their poverty and necessities. I preached publicly on the subject before the Elector, who himself is pious and upright, but the people about him do what they please. Philip Melanchthon and Justus Jonas were lately called in question by the courtiers on account of what I had said, but they replied: "Dr. Luther is old enough, and knows well what he ought to preach."

* * *

Dr. Martin Luther once asked Dr. Hieronymus Weller how he was. He replied, "I am in trouble and sorrow."

"I know how it comes," Dr. Martin Luther answered. "Were you not baptized? Ah, what a great gift of God is baptism, which the Turks and other infidels have not!"

* * * * *

Justus Menius asked Dr. Luther "In what manner a Jew should be baptized?" He replied: "You must fill a tub with water, cause the Jew to take off his clothes, and clothe him in a white garment. He must then sit down in the tub, and you must baptize him under the water. Do it in this fashion; for the ancients, when they were baptized, were clad in white. Perhaps they wore such clothing because it was the custom to attire the dead in white frocks. And baptism is an image of death. I believe that Christ was baptized in this manner by John in Jordan. But if a Jew, not truly pious, came to me for baptism, I would take him to the Elbe Bridge, and hang a stone round his neck, and fling him into the Elbe; for the scoundrels mock us and our religion." Therefore he earnestly counselled Justus Menius not to allow himself to be deceived by the flattering words of the Jews.

Once one who was absent sent a message to Dr. Martin Luther through a friend, and inquired whether baptism might be administered with warm water? Luther replied: "Tell the blockhead that water is water, whether cold or warm."

Christ has given the keys to the Church for consolation, and commanded its servants to employ them to bind the impenitent, and to loose

"With these words he comforted me, and I entered into peace."—*Page* 53.

those who do penance, recognize and confess their sins, and believe that God forgiveth for Christ's sake.

* * * *

The power of God's Word is great, and a brother and a Christian can by means of it lift up and console. The use of the keys and of special absolution in confession is very great, and by it the conscience can be brought to peace, and I would not have it overturned. Under the Papacy I was a poor, sad-hearted monk, and was always in great conflict of spirit. At length I obtained consolation from some words of a brother, who said to me, "You ought to take comfort and hope. Our salvation and blessedness consists in faith upon God in Christ. Why, then, not trust God, who has commanded us to hope?" With these words he comforted me, and I entered into peace.

OF CONFESSION AND ABSOLUTION.

DR. LUTHER was once asked, "If a pastor and confessor were to absolve a woman who had killed her own infant, and a rumour afterwards got abroad of the crime, would the pastor be under an obligation to give evidence before the judge?" Dr. Luther answered, "Most certainly not. Church government ought to be separated from ordinary government, and it is not I that hear confession, but the Lord Christ, and what Christ has not revealed ought not to be revealed by me. I should say, 'I have heard nothing; if Christ has heard anything, let Him speak.' To the woman I would say privately, 'Woman, sin no more.' There was a monk in Venice who absolved a woman who had slain her lover and thrown the body into the water. But the monk was corrupted by money, and betrayed the secret. The woman defended herself by saying that she had received absolution, and she showed the certificate of absolution in the monk's handwriting. The council of Venice recognized it, and condemned the monk to be burned, while the woman was simply expelled from the city. It was a right and rational decision of the council, and the monk deserved to be condemned as a traitor."

THE LORD'S SUPPER.

I KNOW for certain that the words of the institution of the Lord's Supper are true, and I am therefore prepared to defend them against any one. I have never heard any argument against the Lord's Supper that moved me.

Dr. Luther said at table, in the year 1542, "The sacramentarians plague us about charity in their writings, and they say, 'They of Wittenberg have no charity.' When we ask them what charity is, they say that it consists in this, *Ut consentiamus in doctrinâ, et omittamus rixas illas de religione.* We must answer them by saying, Listen, there are two tables in the Ten Commandments—the first and the second; now, charity belongs to the second table. But in the first table the meaning is, *Time Deum, audi verbum ejus.* In the second table we read, *Ama, ama, sis pius in patrem, matrem et proximum.* But in the first, *Si quis diligit plus patrem et matrem quam me, non est me dignus.* The second table says, 'Cherish charity towards parents, towards children, to thy wife, and to thy neighbours.' But in the first table it says, '*Si quis diligit plus patrem et matrem quam me.* Where *ille* comes, there must charity cease."

* * *

Dr. Martin Luther was asked if one who was about to die, and could not obtain the sacrament from the Papists, might take it himself. "No," said he, "since there ought always to be at least two persons present—one who gives, and another who receives. A woman might in case of necessity baptize her child, but the child does not baptize itself."

GOOD WORKS.

THERE was once a monastery which was rich because it gave alms liberally, but when it ceased to give, it became poor. And one came to its gate and begged an alms, and was refused. The beggar said: "Why will you give nothing when I beg for the sake of God?" The porter made answer: "We are poor." The beggar said: "I know the reason of your poverty. You had once two brethren in the monastery. You drove out the one, and the other has secretly gone out after his brother. When the brother *Date* is driven forth, *Dabitur* is likewise lost."

* * *

Dr. Martin Luther once went walking into a neighbouring village with Dr. Jonas and other friends. Dr. Luther gave alms to the poor as they passed through the village. Dr. Jonas also gave some alms, saying: "Who knows what God will give me in return?" Luther laughed and said: "As if God had never given you anything! One should give with simplicity, out of pure love, and willingly."

OF THE DEVIL.

"WHEN the devil comes to torment me by night," said Dr. Martin Luther, "I give him this answer: 'Devil, I must sleep now. It is God's command and ordinance that we work by day and sleep by night.' When he presses hard upon me because of my sins, and accuses me as a great sinner, I treat him with scorn and say, '*Sancte Satane, ora pro nobis;* for thou hast never done any evil, thou alone art holy!

Go to God thyself, and win grace for thyself. *Medice, cura te ipsum.*"

* * *
*

This is the greatest and most difficult temptation of the devil that he says: "God is the enemy of sinners; but thou art a sinner; therefore is God thy enemy." We ought to flatly contradict the first words of this syllogism and conclusion. It is false that God is the enemy of sinners, for Christ says clearly, and by His Father's command: "I am come to save sinners" (Matt. ix. 13). If Satan holds up before thee Sodom and other examples of God's wrath, hold up Christ to him, who became man for our sakes. Had God been the enemy of sinners He would not have given His only-begotten Son for their sakes.

* * *
*

Of the Devil.

The devil gives heaven before sin. After the sin, he torments the conscience and causes despair. Christ does the exact reverse. After sin He gives heaven and a joyful conscience.

* * *

The devil is a sad spirit, and he makes people sad, and therefore cannot endure joyfulness. This is the reason why he flees away at the sound of music as far as he can. He will not remain within the sound of singing, especially of spiritual songs.

* * *

Mention was made of the tempest there was at Nürnberg on February 18, 1533. It began at midnight, and raged so fiercely that four thousand trees fell in the Nürnberg forest, and the roof of the castle was half torn off. There was a fearful wind accompanied with thunder and lightning: so terrible was the storm that men imagined that the last day had come. Dr. Martin Luther remarked that it is the devil who sends such tempests, but the good winds are caused by the good angels. The devil snorts and blows as do the good angels when the good winds come.

***

The devil vexes and deceives the workmen in the mines. He makes them imagine that they see veins of tin and silver when there is nothing there. For when he can bewitch and deceive people on the earth and under the light of the sun, so that they see one thing and think they see another, he can do it still more easily below ground in the mines. I do not deny that tin is sometimes found in the mines, but that is a special gift of God. I never had any fortune in the mines, for Satan did not favour me with that gift of God, and I am well content.

* * * *

It is Satan, I believe, who sends plagues and sore sicknesses upon men; for he is the prince of death. Peter says (Acts x. 38), "Christ healed all who were oppressed of the devil." But Christ did not heal the possessed only, He also gave sight to the blind, made the lame to walk, cleansed the lepers, and caused the deaf to hear. I think, therefore, that sicknesses come from the devil. But he employs natural instruments as a murderer employs a sword, and as God Himself uses natural means to give me life and health, such as sleep, food, and drink. Without means He does not commonly work. So does the devil injure and slay men by using means such as poisoning the air. A physician is God's cobbler, and mends the body; we theologians are the spiritual cobblers and mend what the devil has injured. Our burgomaster once asked me if it was against God's will that we should make use of medicine; for Dr. Carlstadt had been preaching publicly, "If a man is sick he ought not to use medicine, but he should go to God secretly and lay the matter before Him in prayer, and ask that His will should be done." I asked him, "Do you eat when you are hungry?" "Yes," said he. "Then," said I, "you may use medicine, for medicine is God's creature as much as food and drink."

"I ASKED HIM, 'DO YOU EAT WHEN YOU ARE HUNGRY?'"—*Page* 68.

PRAYER.

AS it is the special work of a shoemaker to make shoes, and of a tailor to make coats, so is it the special work of a Christian to pray.

* * *

The prayers of the Churches work great miracles. In my time it has raised three persons from the dead: myself, who have been often dying, my wife Kate, and Philip Melanchthon, who, in the year 1540, lay at the point of death in Weimar. Although deliverance from disease and bodily dangers are but poor miracles, yet ought we to notice them for the sake of those who are weak in the faith. To me it is a much greater miracle that our Lord daily gives baptism in the churches, the sacrament of the altar, and frees and absolves from sin, from death, and damnation. These are to me the great miracles.

* * * *

A question was asked regarding the words of Jeremiah, in which the prophet curses the day on which he was born (Jer. xx. 14). It was asked whether such words were sinful and unchristian. Dr. Martin Luther said, "We have sometimes to waken up our Lord God with such words, or He would not listen to us."

BOOK II.

OF DEATH.

WHEN his daughter lay very sick, Dr. Martin Luther said, "I love her dearly, but dear God, if it is Thy will that she should go hence, I shall willingly give her to Thee." He then said to his daughter, who lay on the bed: "Magdalene, my daughter, willingly thou remainest with thy father, and thou goest willingly to the Father yonder!" She said: "Yes, father dear. As God will." Then said her father,

"My dear little daughter, the spirit is willing, but the flesh is weak."

* * * *

When Magdalene lay in the last agonies, and desired to die, her father fell on his knees before the bed, and, weeping bitterly, prayed that God would deliver her. Then she departed, and fell asleep in her father's arms. The mother was also in the chamber, though farther off, because of her great sorrow. Magdalene's death took place at nine o'clock on Wednesday, the Seventeenth Sunday after Trinity, in the year 1542.

* * * *

The Doctor repeated often the words: "Willingly would I have retained her, for she was very dear to me, but His will be done. For her nothing better could have happened!" Master Philip then said, "The love of parents is an image of the love of God impressed upon the human heart. If the love of God to the human race is as great as the love of parents to children, as Scripture says it is, then is it a great love indeed."

* * *

When she lay in her coffin, Dr. Luther said: "Ah, dear Lene, thou shalt rise again, and shine like a star, yea, like the sun! I am joyful in spirit, but the flesh is sorrowful!"

* * *

When the people came to help to bury the dead, Luther addressed them according to custom, and said: "My trouble makes you sorrowful, rather ought you to rejoice. I have sent a saint to heaven, yes, a living saint. Oh, that we all could have such a death!"

On the night before Magdalene died, Luther's wife had a dream, in which she saw two fair young men, gaily attired, come to fetch Magdalene to her wedding. When Philip Melanchthon came in the morning into the cloister he asked: "How is your daughter?" Then the mother told him her dream; but he was affrighted, and said to the others: "These young men were the dear angels who shall come to fetch this maiden to her true marriage in the kingdom of heaven."

OF THE RESURRECTION OF THE DEAD AND LIFE ETERNAL.

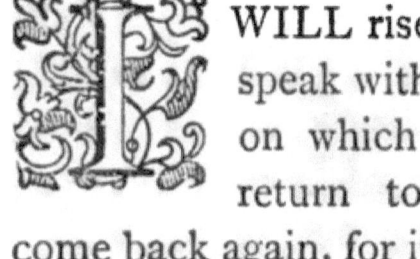WILL rise again, and again speak with you. The finger on which this ring is shall return to me. All shall come back again, for it is written (2 Pet. iii. 3), God will create "a new heaven and a new earth in which dwelleth

righteousness." That will be no empty or indolent realm. There will be pure joy, and rejoicing throughout it; for heaven and earth will not be dry, unfruitful plains of sand. When man is joyful, every little tree rejoiceth, yea, every fair little flower and shrub; but when he is sorrowful, scarce can a tree hold up its head. Heaven and earth will be renewed, and we believers shall all at once become a mighty multitude. One asked Dr. Martin Luther, "Will there be dogs and other beasts in the future kingdom of heaven?" "Yes, assuredly," he said, "for the earth will not be a lonely, empty desert. But they will no longer eat one another as do the toads, serpents, and other poisonous creatures, which on account of original sin became poisonous and dangerous. There will they be not only harmless, but loving and playful, and we shall amuse ourselves with them."

Dr. Severus said, "Many doubt concerning the article of the resurrection of the ungodly." Dr. Luther answered, "I have spoken of it fully in my writing on the fifteenth chapter of the First Epistle to the Corinthians." Master John Matheson, Dr. Luther's companion at table, then said, "Sir Doctor, in the Creed there are, first, the words *remissio peccatorum*, afterwards follow the words *carnis resurrectio*, which seems to show that those alone shall rise from the dead who have received forgiveness of sins." Dr. Luther said, "There are clear proofs in the Scriptures for the resurrection of all the dead, such as John v. 28, 29; Matt. xxv. 32."

OF MARRIAGE.

LUCAS CRANACH the elder had painted a picture of Dr. Martin Luther's wife. And when the picture was hung upon the wall, Luther looked at it and said: "I shall have the husband painted also, and shall send the two pictures to the council at Mantua, and ask the holy Fathers assembled there, whether they like the married state or celibacy for the clergy."

* * *
 *

On the day of St. Martin, Dr. Martin Luther celebrated his birthday, and many learned men were invited to his table, among others Dr. Jonas, Dr. Caspar Creuziger, and Philip Melanchthon. Before supper Master Ambrose Bernd requested that the Doctor's niece Magdalene should be given him in marriage. Dr. Martin Luther said: "Dear friend, God has entrusted the maiden to me, and to Him I am responsible. May God give His blessing and benediction so that you may live a Christian life together!" Then was the company joyful. Afterwards Dr. Luther spoke of wooing, and of that freedom which had been granted a newly-married bridegroom by Moses, otherwise a stern and hard lawgiver, when he enacted that the bridegroom should be freed from public duties for a whole year.

In the year 1538, on November 22, Master Ambrose Bernd had a conversation aside with his betrothed. When Dr. Martin Luther observed them he laughed, and said: "I marvel that a bridegroom and bride have so much to say to one another, and that they never grow weary. But we must not vex them; they have privileges above all law and custom."

* * * *

Mr. G. has married a rich wife, and has sold his freedom. Commonly it happens this way. When a poor fellow marries a rich woman, if he says anything that offends her, she immediately opens her mouth and upbraids him, saying: "You good-for-nothing fellow! you would have been a beggar had I not married you!" Marriages made for the sake of wealth are commonly accursed; rich women, for the most part, are proud, cross, and negligent, and waste more than they bring.

* * * * *

On New Year's Day Dr. Martin Luther's child wept and screamed so that it was impossible to quiet it; the Doctor and his wife were much troubled for a whole hour. And he said, "There are tiresome things and troubles in marriage, and that is why men avoid it and remain unmarried. We are afraid of the whims of women, the howling and screaming of children, of expense, and bad neighbours; and therefore we wish to be free lords and to do whatever we please. It is for this reason that none of the Fathers ever said anything good regarding marriage. But God of His grace has again by His word, before the day of judgment, given their true place to government, to the preaching of the gospel, and to marriage."

* * *

Dr. Luther sometimes laughed at his Kate for her gossip and chatter; and he once said, "Did you say the Lord's Prayer before preaching such a long sermon?" But women do not pray before they preach, for if they did they would leave off preaching; or if God heard them at once, He would forbid them to preach.

* * *

Were I to marry again I should carve an obedient woman out of stone. For I despair otherwise of finding obedience in women.

OF THE JEWS.

THE Jews are the most miserable of all the peoples on earth : they are everywhere plagued, and are scattered in many lands, and have no certain dwelling-place. They have neither country, nation, nor government, and yet they suffer everything, and wait with great eagerness, and comfort one another by saying, "It will soon be better with us."

"If I were a Jew the Pope should never persuade me to his idolatry; I should rather be broken on the wheel ten times. The Papacy, with its abominations and its idolatries, has been a great stumbling-block to the Jews. My belief is, that were the Jews to hear our preaching, and how we handle the words of the Old Testament, many would be won. By disputing with them we make them more fierce and stiff-necked, and they are by nature proud and presumptuous. But if one or two of their rabbis and chief men fell off from them, then a change might come, for they are almost tired of waiting."

* * * *

There are many Jews in Frankfort-on-the-Main, and they live together in a single street, in which every house is crowded. They are

Of the Jews.

obliged to wear yellow rings on their clothes that they may be known. They possess neither houses nor lands, only movable property. They can only lend money upon houses or land at a great risk.

* * * *

There is no doubt that in remote times a great number of Jews fled to Italy and Germany and settled there. The eloquent heathen Cicero complains of the superstition of the Jews, and of their numbers in Italy. We can trace their footsteps through the whole of Germany. There is no city, no village, in Germany that has not Jewish names and streets. It is said that there were Jews living in Regensburg long before the birth of Christ. It was a mighty nation.

* * * *

"There once came to me," said

Dr. Martin Luther, "two Jewish rabbis, and begged of me letters of safe conduct. They would have been satisfied with the letters I gave them, had I omitted from them the word *Tola*, that is, Jesus the crucified. They must blaspheme the name 'Jesus,' and the hymn *Jesus is risen* is always obnoxious to them. All other hymns pall upon us after a time, but every year we must sing afresh of the resurrection of Jesus." Another Jew said, "Thousands of innocent men have been murdered, but no one now speaks of them; but Jesus the Crucified One must always be thought of—His death it seems impossible to forget."

* * *
*

A Jew, who wished to be baptized and to receive the Christian faith, made confession to a priest and said, "Before baptism I should like to go to Rome and see the Head of the Christian world." The priest endeavoured to dissuade him, for he feared that if the Jew beheld all the wickedness and folly of Rome, he might be repelled from Christianity. But the Jew persisted, and he travelled to Rome, and beheld there many abominations; but he returned to the priest and asked for baptism, saying, "I will now willingly worship the God of the Christians, for He is patient enough. If He can bear with such wickedness and villainy as is to be seen in Rome, He can bear with the villainy and vice of the whole world."

OF ECCLESIASTICAL LEGENDS.

A FRIEND once asked Dr. Luther, "What legends are canonical, that is to say, in harmony with Scripture, and what apocryphal, or not in harmony with Scripture?" He replied, "Very few are pure. The legends of the martyrs are the least corrupt, for they bore witness to their faith with their blood. The legends of monks, especially of

the hermits who lived apart from men, are horrible, and are filled with lying miracles and foolish stories about unnatural abstinence and torture of their bodies. I esteem greatly those saints, of whom nothing marvellous is recorded, who lived like other people, without pretence, and did not seek to make themselves notorious."

* *
*
*

Dr. Martin Luther preached about St. Christopher on the day of that saint and said, "It is not a history but a story invented by the Greeks, who were a wise and ingenious people. Its purpose is to show what the life of a Christian should be, and how it fares with him. St. Christopher is a tall, strong man, who bears upon his shoulders the child Jesus. But he finds the child so heavy that he stoops under his burden as he walks through the wild, raging sea. The sea is the world, and the waves are the tyrants and wicked gangs by whose malice he is all but destroyed. But he supports himself by a great tree, as upon a staff; that is, upon God's word. On the other side of the sea stands an old man with a lantern, in which there burns a bright light; this means the writings of the prophets. By it he guides himself and comes unharmed to shore, that is, to the life eternal. By his side there is a wallet, which contains fish and bread, and that shows that God will not suffer Christians to perish of hunger in this world, although the world would gladly be rid of them. It is a beautiful Christian poem."

THE WORLD AND ITS WAYS.

GOD might have left the world uncreated, but He created it that He might display His honour and power. We must not ask our Lord God and say, *Quare hoc facis?* We ought to perform that which is commanded us, and not to say, *Quare?* We must accept it that our Lord God is more pious than we. What is good comes from God; what is evil comes from the devil. Man uses his goods and his mind against God rather than for his own honour. Hence it comes that a man's friends are his greatest enemies.

* * *
*

The world will never allow itself to be governed by laws and rules. It is very averse to trammels and reins. It would be free as a bird, as free as the irregular verb in Donatus, *sum, es, est, eram, fui,* &c. It cannot be conjugated like another word. It goes now to one side, and now to another, like a meadow. There are also *Defectiva,* or verbs wanting in some of their parts, as the book in the schools *Bellum Grammaticale* is called. It is thus with the world which will not submit itself to law or discipline. It is the devil's bride who rides and drives it, so that it does from the heart only that which the bridegroom wills. We must let it remain *sum, es, est*, and not attempt to transform it into *sum, sus, sut*, for it is a self-willed word.

*
* *
*

The world is an assemblage of people who receive from God nothing but benefits, and render back thanklessness and blasphemy to the Giver.

*
* *
*

The peasants are not worthy of the fruits which the earth bears for them. I thank our God more for a single tree or a plant than do all the peasants for their fields. Then spake Philip Melanchthon and said, "Ah, Sir Doctor, but you must make some exceptions as Adam, Noah, Abraham, and Isaac who went forth to his fields that he might meditate on God's gifts in the creatures" (Gen. xxiv.).

Human reason leads either to despair or to presumption. When she despairs, she dies *sine crux et lux*. But when she is exalted, she goes forth and is deceived.

* * * *

I have often wondered what led the heathen to say so many beautiful things of death which is so fearful and hateful. But when I consider the world, I wonder no more; for there were so many stupid scoundrels in authority in the world who did them evil, that they had nothing to threaten them with but death. If the heathen regarded death so little, yea, held it in honour, how much more should we Christians? for the poor people knew less than nothing of the life eternal; but we know of it. But we are filled with fear and terror when any one talks to us of death. The cause of that is our sins, and we must confess that we 'live worse than the heathen; and we cannot rightly complain, for the greater the sin, the more fearful is death.

* * * *

The physician of the Bishop of Mainz, who fell off from the Gospel to Papacy and became a Mameluke, once said: "I will place Christ behind the door for a time till I become rich, afterwards will I bring Him forth again." And an ungodly usurer said: "If you are one who walks in fear of death, you will never become rich." Such ungodly and blasphemous speeches deserve and will receive the most severe punishment.

* * * *

It is a marvel, and a very scandalous thing, that after the pure doctrine of the gospel is again come to light, through the special grace and revelation of God, the world has become worse. Every one now makes Christian freedom a plea for the indulgence of his own will, just as if he had a right to do whatever pleases him. The kingdom of the devil and the Pope, as far as external government is concerned, is best for the world; for by them the world will be ruled by means of strict rules and laws, by superstition and vain imaginings. The teaching of the grace of God makes it more wicked; for when it hears there is another world, it makes peace with this world, and leaves the Lord God to take care of the other. They are satisfied if they have only pleasant days, honours, and possessions as the Roman Popes and Cardinals have. A rich Cardinal died once in Rome and left behind him a great sum of money. In the coffer which contained his money he left a bull. The coffer was opened after his death, and they found these words inscribed upon the parchment :

Dum potui, rapui ; rapiatis quando potestis.

Oh, how must the Cardinal have died, and what a fate must his have been !

OF PRINCES AND RULERS

GOVERNMENT is a sign of Divine grace. Its existence shows the mercy of God, and that He has no pleasure in murdering, killing, and strangling. The magistrate is like a fish net which is placed in a stream when fish are to be taken. But God is the troubler of the water who drives the fish into the net. For when a thief, robber, adulterer, or murderer is ripe, God chases him into the net; that is, He brings it about that he is taken and punished by the magistrate. For it is written in the Psalms: "God is Judge upon earth."

* * *

Rulers ought to give honour to the gospel, and to hold it high with both hands, for it upholds them and ennobles their position and office, so that they know what their calling is, and can perform its duties with a good conscience. In former times under the Papacy princes and lords were afraid of shedding blood, and of punishing robbers, murderers, and thieves: they did not rightly distinguish between the private person and him who performs a public duty. The executioner had to do penance and to beg forgiveness from the condemned criminal when he was about to execute his office, as if he had been doing wrong; whereas it is his proper office which God hath appointed. St. Paul says, "He beareth not the sword in vain." When the magistrate punishes, it is God Himself who is punishing.

* * * *

Duke Frederick, the Elector of Saxony, was very reluctant to punish malefactors, especially the poor thieves. "Ah!" said he, "it is easy to take away life, but we cannot give it back again." And Duke John, the Elector of Saxony, was in the habit of saying about a criminal: "Ah! he will reform and become a good man yet." Through all this weakness the land has become full of scoundrels. The princes were also persuaded by the monks that it was their duty to be gracious and kind. But magistrates, princes, and lords must not be soft and yielding.

On one occasion a boy of eighteen years was brought before a judge for theft. The judge was anxious to save him from the gallows, and to release him because of his youth. But the prisoner said, "Make an end of me at once, for that is my destiny. If you release me, I shall assuredly return to the work of stealing." Dr. Luther then repeated the old proverb, "A thief is nowhere better than on the gallows, a monk in the cloister, and a fish in the water." He had begged off, he said, several from the gallows, but after a few days they stole again and were executed after all. Joab's counsel was much better than that of King David.

Dr. Martin Luther was on a certain occasion the guest of the Duke Ernst of Lüneburg, and of the Duke

William of Mecklenburg. Duke Ernst was a pious prince, and he complained of the drunken and licentious life led at courts, where, he said, men eat and drink all day, and yet pretend to be Christians. Dr. Luther replied, "The princes and lords ought to interpose." But Duke Ernst said, "Ah, Doctor, we lead the same life ourselves. If we did not, it would have ceased long ago." Meaning that the intemperance of princes is the cause of the intemperance of the people. When the abbot throws the dice, the whole convent will play.

* * *

Dr. Philip Melanchthon said on one occasion to Dr. Luther, as they sat at table, that he heard in his youth that during a Diet of the empire certain princes were boasting of the riches and advantages of their realms.

The Elector of Saxony said that he had mountains of silver in his land, and mines from which he derived great revenues. The Elector Palatine praised his wine which came from his vineyards on the Rhine. When it came to the turn of Eberhard, of Würtemberg, to speak, he said, "I am indeed but a poor prince, and am not to be compared with either of you; but I have also a precious jewel in my country; for should I at any time ride astray in my country and find myself alone in the fields, I could safely sleep on the bosom of any one of my subjects." When the other two princes heard this, they confessed that his was the richest and most precious jewel.

OF THE USE OF LEARNING.

WISDOM, understanding, learning, and the pen govern the world. If God in His anger were to take away all the learned from the world, men would become wild beasts; there would be no understanding or wit — nothing but robbery, stealing, murder, adultery. The mob would like that there were no wise and learned men left, for then would they live as they pleased. If that were so, the world would go to ruin, for without understanding wisdom even Turks and Tartars could not live. Where there are men, there must be law and order.

OF COMEDIES.

DR. JOHN CELLARIUS asked the counsel of Dr. Martin Luther on the following point. There was a learned schoolmaster who had caused a comedy of Terence to be acted. But many were offended, and thought that it did not become a Christian man to concern himself with the plays of heathen poets. Dr. Luther replied, "It ought not to be forbidden to boys in school to play comedies; they ought rather to be permitted. Firstly, because it affords them practice in the Latin tongue. Secondly, because in comedies characters are well portrayed, and people are taught the conduct becoming in various positions in life. As in a mirror, they see in plays what is becoming in a servant, what in a lord, what becomes the young, and what the old. Christians should not entirely flee from comedies because now and then there are coarse matters in them. For the same reason we might cease to read the Bible."

OF THE POWER OF MUSIC.

THE fairest and most glorious gift of God is music. It drives away the spirit of sadness as we see in the case of Saul. Kings, princes, and great lords ought to give their support to music; for it becomes potentates to maintain noble arts and laws. Music is a discipline, it is an instructress, and it makes people milder and gentler, more moral and more reasonable. Even the bad players do this service, that by their means we recognize what is good music; for we never recognize the white better than when the black is placed beside it.

※ ※ ※ ※

Music is a fair and glorious gift of God, and takes a place next to theology. I would not part with my small skill in music for much. The young ought continually to accustom themselves to this art, for it makes people cultivated and clever.

OF SINGING.

SINGING is the best art and custom. It has nothing to do with this world. Singers are not care-laden people, but joyful, and they drive away care with their songs.

* * *

While they were singing Passion music Dr. Martin Luther listened with great attention to it and said, " Music is a fair and sweet gift of God. It has often given to me new life, and inspired me with a desire to preach. Saint Augustine had a conscientious scruple about it. When he heard music with pleasure, and was made joyful by it, he would afterwards weep as if he had committed a sin. He was, however, a noble, pious man. If he lived now he would be on our side. But Saint Jerome would condemn us."

OF GERMANY.

DR. MARTIN LUTHER and Philip Melanchthon journeyed to Torgau on April 3, 1537, and they spoke together of various matters. Philip praised the chronicle of Cornelius Tacitus, who lived in the days of the Emperor Caligula, and wrote beautifully of Germany, which he praised because of its steadfastness and fidelity. For then were the Germans steadfast, and kept troth, especially in marriage, in which they excelled all other nations. "Yes," said Dr. Martin Luther, "it was so among the ancient Germans, and they were noble men; but now, alas! in these last times have they sadly fallen off."

* * * * *

Germany is like a fair, strong steed, which has all the fodder it needs. What is wanting is a good rider. Germany has strength and people, but it wants a good head and ruler.

* * * * *

In the year 1538, on the 8th of December, there came a pious, honourable matron from Magdeburg to Dr. Martin Luther. She was a very tall woman, and her daughter was equally so, and her son was a head taller than

Master Anthony Lauterbach, the deacon of Wittenberg, who is a very tall man. Then said Dr. Martin Luther, "You may see in these an example of the old German bodies. They who lived long ago were like giants; we have become pigmies and dwarfs."

* * *

I believe that England is a part of Germany. The people there speak the Saxon speech as in Westphalia and the Netherlands, although it is very much corrupted. I believe that the Germans in ancient times passed over to England and settled there.

* * *

If I were to travel much, I should like best to travel in Bavaria and in Swabia; for the people there are friendly and good-humoured, hospitable to travellers and strangers, and they give them good entertainment for their money. The Hessians and the dwellers in Meissen do also to a certain extent, but they are very eager for money. But the Saxons are very unfriendly and discourteous, and give neither good words nor good eating. You see here in Wittenberg what an unfriendly people they are. Expect neither honesty, nor politeness, nor religion here. No citizen of Wittenberg will allow his son to study, although they have a noble example before them in the number of stranger students and guests who flock to their city.

OF LANGUAGES.

THE Greeks have good and charming words, but they have no sentence. Their language is friendly and gracious, but it is not rich in proverbs. The Hebrew language is simple, but majestic and glorious. Simple and few it is in its words, but there is much behind them. It is pure, and does not go a-begging for words to other languages, but preserves its own colour. The Greeks, Latins, and Germans beg words, and their languages have many compounds. I am not master either of Hebrew or of Greek, but nevertheless I think I could encounter a Hebrew or a Greek pretty well. The languages alone will not make a theologian; they are only helps. If a man is to speak of a matter, he must first of all know and understand the thing itself.

*   *   *   *

I have no special German speech, but I use the common German speech so that both High German and Low German may understand me. I speak after the Saxon Chancery which is followed by all princes and kings in Germany and by the Imperial towns.

*   *   *   *

The languages are fair and glorious gifts of God ; but men pay no heed to them. They are preserved by God alone.

OF THE SCHOOLS AND UNIVERSITIES OF GERMANY.

THE universities of Germany are not very old. Fulda and certain rich monasteries were the first universities, and these by preaching and teaching instructed the youth in religion and in the useful arts. Had it not been for them the youth would have remained uncared for. But after the monasteries became rich, they put this work from them, and the studies were corrupted.

* * *
*

In the year 1539, on the 18th day of January, in the evening, a comet was visible at Wittenberg. It was seen with great wonder by Dr. Martin Luther, Jonas, Philip Melanchthon, Milich, and Erasmus the astronomer. Dr. Martin Luther said: "I will prophesy of the wrath of God against Germany, not from the heavens, but from theology and the Word of God. It is impossible that Germany should escape without punishment. A great calamity will overtake it; for God is constantly tempted to destroy us. The godly will perish with the ungodly. Let us only pray, and not despise God and His Word. Although we are all alike great sinners, yet is forgiveness of sins and eternal life promised to us in the Word,

"It was seen with great wonder by Luther."—*Page* 128.

and Turk and Emperor help us to it. They will not harm us, but will rather help us on our way, but it grieves me on account of posterity, for they will be brought again out of the light into the darkness."

OF THE TURKS.

DR. MARTIN LUTHER wrote once to a great lord who had been made commander-in-chief in war against the Turks. He counselled him to lay to heart that he had four enemies with whom to reckon. He had not to contend with flesh and blood, but with the devil, who was the first enemy. Secondly, he had to reckon with the Turks. Thirdly, with the anger of God.

Fourthly, with his own sins and those of his people. He ought to think of these things, humble himself, and pray to God for help.

OF HEROES AND WISE MEN OF ANTIQUITY.

DR. MARTIN LUTHER spoke of the actions of heroes and great men, such as Alexander, Augustus, Hannibal, Pompey, and the like. "All," he said, "are not fit for the work of ruling men. Warriors think of nothing but victory, and how to hold the field, and they bestow no thought upon good government, nor consider how a land

and a people are to be well ruled. Such were Scipio, Hannibal, Alexander, and Julius Cæsar. But Augustus gave heed to government, and considered how it was to be carried on."

* * *
*

Cicero is greatly superior to Aristotle in philosophy and in teaching; the *Officia* of Cicero are greatly superior to the *Ethica* of Aristotle. And although Cicero was involved in the cares of government, and had much on his shoulders, he greatly excels Aristotle, who was a lazy ass, and cared for nothing but money and possessions, and comfortable, easy days. Cicero handled the greatest and best questions in his philosophy, such as: Is there a God? What is God? Does He give heed to the actions of men? Is the soul immortal? &c. Aristotle is a good and skilful dialectician, who has observed the right and orderly method in teaching, but the kernel of matters has he not touched. Let those who wish to see a true philosophy read Cicero. Cicero was a wise and industrious man, and he suffered much and accomplished much. I hope that our Lord God will be gracious to him and to the like of him. Of this we are not entitled to speak with certainty. Although the revealed Word must abide, " He who believeth, and is baptized, shall be saved" (Mark xvi. 16), yet is it possible that God may dispense with it in the case of the heathen. There will be a new heaven and a new earth, much larger than the present; and He can give to every one according to His good pleasure.

* * *
*

Dr. Martin Luther praised very highly the fables of Æsop, and said:

"They ought to be translated into German, and well arranged. It is a book not made by one man, but by many great men at various times. It is of the special grace of God that Cato's little book and the fables of Æsop are used in the schools. As far as I am able to judge, there are no better books than Cato's writings and the fables of Æsop."

OF THE FATHERS AND DOCTORS OF THE CHURCH.

THE Church Fathers wrote many good and useful things. Their writings should be read, however, with discrimination, and we ought not to accept and justify all that they say until we have applied to it the test of the Word of God. Hilary and Augustine wrote much that was good and admirable of the Holy Trinity and Justification, and also of heretics. Nazianzene nothing. Gregory is a monk, Cyprian a pious man and an orator. Tertullian and Eusebius write histories only. Lactantius, as Augustine says, writes of strange things. In peace have they accomplished nothing, but they were mighty in strife. Bernard loved Jesus as much as any man; but in controversy, when he enters the list with foes, he is Bernard no more.

* * *
*

Saint Ambrose was a pious, God-fearing, and courageous man. When his enemies, the servants of the Emperor, commanded him to come out of the Church and to give up the rights and property of the Church, he lifted up his head and said, "See, here I stand, and I am ready to die." He

Doctors of the Church.

was a man of noble, joyful, and steadfast soul. Although the Emperor Theodosius was usually a pious man, Saint Ambrose drove him out of choir and church, and placed him under excommunication, because he had acted with violence, and had committed a great massacre in a city, sparing neither maidens nor children.

* * *
*

Jerome ought not to be reckoned among the teachers of the Church, for he was a heretic. I believe, however, that he attained to salvation through his faith in Christ. He says nothing of Christ, for it is only His name that he has on his lips. I know no teacher to whom I am so hostile as Jerome; for he writes of nothing but fasts and meats and virginity. Had he spoken of the works of faith, it had been something; but he teaches nothing either of hope, or of love, or of the works of faith.

* * *
*

Saint Augustine was painted in a book as a monk with a monk's cowl. Dr. Luther said, "They do the holy man injustice, for he led an ordinary life like any other citizen, and had silver spoons and cups. He was as a man among other people, and did not live the monstrous monkish life. But the Papists invented the fable in order to defend their own errors."

* * *
*

"The Master of Sentences," Peter Lombard, was a very diligent man, and of a lofty understanding, and he wrote much that is excellent. He could have been a great and eminent doctor of the churches, had he devoted himself with earnestness to Holy Scripture.

But he brought confusion into his book by means of the useless questions which he raised. Yet there were fine heads in those days, and they had no such favourable times as we have.

www.ingramcontent.com/pod-product-compliance
Lightning Source LLC
Chambersburg PA
CBHW030347170426
43202CB00010B/1278